Going to Yellowstone

by Peter and Connie Roop

Old Faithful Geyser, September 15, 1895

FARCOUNTRY
PRESS

Helena, Montana

About the Authors

Together, Peter and Connie Roop have written more than one hundred books for children, on topics from science to history. Their books have received numerous awards.

Connie, a geologist by training, teaches high school environmental science. She was named Appleton's Teacher of the Year in 2001. Peter taught elementary school for twenty-five years before becoming a full-time author and speaker. Peter sees thousands of students each year during his school visits across America. He was selected Wisconsin State Teacher of the Year in 1987.

For Tom, Janet, and Stuart, who know and love Yellowstone so well. Thanks for your friendship and support!

ISBN 10: 1-56037-361-X
ISBN 13: 978-1-56037-361-2
© 2005 by Farcountry Press
Text © 2005 by Peter and Connie Roop

For more information about our books, write Farcountry Press, P.O. Box 5630, Helena, MT 59604; call (800) 821-3874; or visit www.farcountrypress.com.

Created, produced, and designed in the United States.
Manufactured by
Samhwa Printing Co., Ltd
237-10 Kuro3-Don, Juro-Ku
Seoul, Korea
June 2012
Printed in Korea.

16   15   14   13   12   4   5   6   7   8

Photo and Illustration Credits

1916 Yellowstone Park map courtesy Wyoming State Parks and Cultural Resources Department
front cover, photo by Fred Pflughoft; illustrations by Bob Everton
back cover, William Henry Jackson painting courtesy Department of the Interior Museum; bighorn sheep photo by John C. Eriksson
p. 1, photo courtesy Haynes Foundation Collection, Montana Historical Society
p. 3, photo courtesy Haynes Foundation Collection, Montana Historical Society
p. 4, illustrations by Bob Everton
p. 5, illustration by Bob Everton, photo by Fred Pflughoft
p. 6, illustrations by Bob Everton, photo by Larry Mayer, Billings Gazette
p. 7, "Annie" courtesy U.S. Geological Survey Photographic Archive; illustration by Bob Everton
p. 8, black-and-white photo courtesy U.S. Geological Survey Photographic Archive; color photo by Fred Pflughoft
p. 9, obsidian points photo by Fred Pflughoft; black-and-white NPS Photo
p. 10, Bighorn sheep photo by John L. Hinderman; Sheepeater woman photo courtesy Montana Historical Society Photo Archives; Obsidian Cliff photo courtesy U.S. Geological Survey Photographic Archive
p. 11, illustrations by Bob Everton; Thomas Moran painting courtesy U.S. Department of the Interior Museum, Washington D.C.
p. 12, "Castle Geyser" by Thomas Moran courtesy The Library of Congress; odometer and "Valley of the Yellowstone" photos by William Henry Jackson courtesy U.S. Geological Survey Photographic Archive
p. 13, Thomas Moran portrait and Washburn Expedition map courtesy NPS Photo Archives; William Henry Jackson portrait and Hayden Expedition courtesy U.S. Geological Survey Photographic Archive; William Henry Jackson painting courtesy U.S. Department of the Interior Museum, Washington D.C.
p. 14, Grant portrait courtesy The Library of Congress; Roosevelt Arch courtesy Montana Magazine
p. 15, photo by Fred Pflughoft
p. 16, photo by David Peterson
p. 17, illustration by Bob Everton; photo by Fred Pflughoft
p. 18, illustration by Bob Everton; color photo by Fred Pflughoft; black-and-white photo courtesy NPS Historic Photograph Collection
p. 19, Grand Prismatic Spring by David Peterson; thermophiles NPS Photo
p. 20, mud pot by David Peterson; fumaroles by Chuck Haney
p. 21, photo by Fred Pflughoft

p. 22, photo by Fred Pflughoft
p. 23, photo by Fred Pflughoft
p. 24, Elk cow and calf NPS Photo; Liberty Cap photo by Fred Pflughoft; Fort Yellowstone courtesy Haynes Foundation Collection, Montana Historical Society
p. 25, photo by David Peterson; inset photo courtesy Montana Historical Society
p. 26, black-and-white photo courtesy U.S. Geological Survey Photographic Archive; color photo by Fred Pflughoft
p. 27, photo by Fred Pflughoft
p. 28, photo by John L. Hinderman; illustration by Bob Everton
p. 29, osprey photo by John C. Eriksson; illustration by Bob Everton; aerial of wolves NPS Photo
p. 30, wolf release NPS Photo; illustrations by Bob Everton; coyote photo by John C. Eriksson
p. 31, photo by John C. Eriksson
p. 32, photo by John C. Eriksson; illustration by Bob Everton
p. 33, photos by Fred Pflughoft
p. 34, illustration by Bob Everton; bighorn sheep and moose by John C. Eriksson; elk photo by Fred Pflughoft
p. 35, Bull elk and fringed gentian photo by Fred Pflughoft; elk herd photo by John L. Hinderman; illustration by Bob Everton
p. 36, Trumpeter swan photo by John L. Hinderman; sandhill crane photo by Fred Pflughoft
p. 37, illustration by Bob Everton; photo by John L. Hinderman
p. 38, illustration by Bob Everton; photo by John C. Eriksson
p. 39, photo by Larry Mayer, Billings Gazette
p. 40, photo by Larry Mayer, Billings Gazette; satellite image courtesy USGS EROS Data Center
p. 41, photo by Larry Mayer, Billings Gazette
p. 42, photo by Bob Zellar, Billings Gazette
p. 43, fireweed photo by Fred Pflughoft; new lodgepole pine shoots NPS Photo; elk calf photo by Bob Zellar, Billings Gazette
p. 44, illustration by Bob Everton; photo by Fred Pflughoft; black-and-white photo courtesy Haynes Foundation Collection, Montana Historical Society
p. 45, photo by Fred Pflughoft; black-and-white photo courtesy Montana Historical Society
p. 46, black-and-white photo courtesy Haynes Foundation Collection, Montana Historical Society; photos by Fred Pflughoft
p. 47, arch ceremony and stagecoach photo NPS Photo Archives; arch inscription NPS Photo
p. 48, soldier photo courtesy NPS Historic Photograph Collection; photo by Fred Pflughoft; black-and-white photo courtesy Haynes Foundation Collection, Montana Historical Society

Table of Contents

Boat Landing, Yellowstone Lake, circa 1908

Yellowstone, Land of Changes

Yellowstone National Park is a land of changes. The geysers, lakes, meadows, and mountains that visitors enjoy today haven't always been there.

What we see in Yellowstone now is relatively new in terms of how the earth is continually changing.

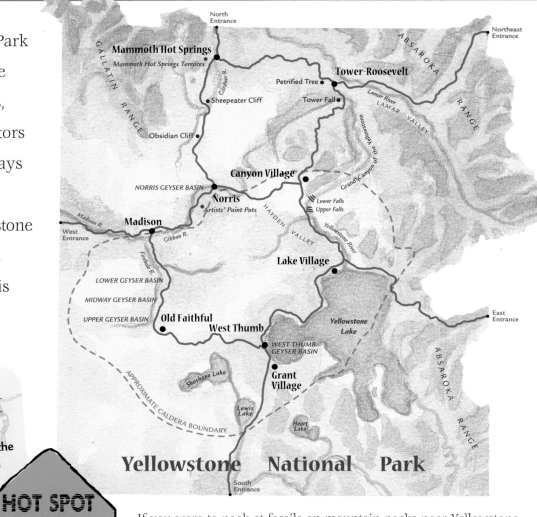

Yellowstone National Park

Nature's Hot Spot

Geologists, scientists who study the earth, tell us that around 15 million years ago the rock under Yellowstone began to heat up. A **"hot spot"** was growing under the region.

Geologists estimate that there are about forty hot spots around the globe. These hot spots are formed by rising plumes of the earth's hot core approaching the surface. For example, Hawaii's volcanoes were created by a hot spot in the Pacific Ocean. Geologists think that a hot spot formed under Yellowstone around 2 million years ago.

This hot spot still fuels Yellowstone's steaming, hissing, erupting marvels.

If you were to peek at fossils on mountain peaks near Yellowstone, you would find **trilobites** and other **ocean animals**. These animals lived under the seas that flooded much of today's western United States, including Yellowstone, for about 400 million years. Instead of bison grazing and wolves hunting, trilobites were crawling in Yellowstone.

Around 65 million years ago when dinosaurs were dying out, the seas retreated. Yellowstone wasn't a thousand miles away from the Pacific Ocean, as it is today. Instead, Yellowstone was the western edge of North America.

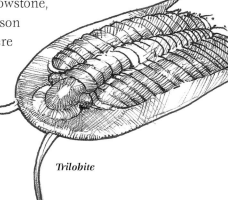

Trilobite

Petrified tree

Yellowstone was much warmer and wetter then, too. Tropical trees like breadfruit and avocado flourished. Hickory, dogwood, and sycamore also grew in Yellowstone.

Around this time Yellowstone's land began rising. **Volcanoes** erupted, burying the land with layer after layer of volcanic ash. Redwood forests similar to those now growing in California were buried in the ash while still standing. Over time, these trees were fossilized or petrified—creating one of the largest **petrified forests** in the world. These petrified trees can be seen in cliffs in the Lamar Valley. At some places, their 50-million-year-old rocky roots still hold trees upright.

Around 20 million years ago, Yellowstone's pine forests began to grow.

Yellowstone Explodes!

The Big Bang

One day, around 2 million years ago, Yellowstone blew its top. A volcanic explosion created a crater nearly 50 miles wide! This crater, called the Huckleberry Ridge Caldera, reached from the center of Yellowstone into Idaho. This huge explosion ejected 2,400 times as much ash as the Mount St. Helens eruption in 1980.

As big as the blast was, scientists estimate that the explosion probably lasted less than a day, maybe even a few minutes.

DANGER BIG BANG

Kaboom Again!

Things had barely settled down when, 1.3 million years ago, Yellowstone exploded again. This explosion, called Island Park, was bigger than the 1815 volcanic eruption in Indonesia, the biggest eruption ever recorded.

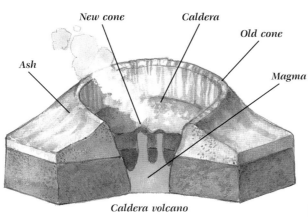

New cone   Caldera
                    Old cone
Ash
                    Magma

Caldera volcano

Last But Not Least

Lava Creek, Yellowstone's last volcanic eruption, occurred 640,000 years ago. Geologists think that this last blast rivaled the Huckleberry Ridge explosion. Ash from Lava Creek has been found north in Canada, south in Mexico, east in Iowa and west in California. At least twenty states show signs of Yellowstone's blast from the past.

CANADA ↑
MEXICO ↓
IOWA →
← CALIFORNIA

Will Yellowstone Explode Again?

Scientists studying Yellowstone say yes! They don't know when, but based on Yellowstone's three ancient eruptions and the magma chamber still underneath the Park, they feel sure that one day in the future Yellowstone will explode again.

What's Left?

Today we can see evidence of these massive volcanic explosions in what remains of their **calderas.** Each of Yellowstone's violent volcanic eruptions left a caldera or crater. Roughly circular in shape, each one was formed after a volcano blew millions of tons of molten rock, gas, and ash into the air. When this material was ejected, the volcano collapsed, creating a caldera. The edges of these holes are the caldera rims. Cracks in the caldera floor opened and red-hot rhyolite lava flooded the caldera. Many of these rhyolite flows are evident in the colorful rocks of the Grand Canyon of the Yellowstone River. These lava flows also formed the relatively flat parts of central Yellowstone National Park, called the Yellowstone Plateau. Hot water pushing up through the rhyolite has created Yellowstone's many thermal features.

One of the best views of the caldera rims is from the top of **Mt. Washburn.**

Yellowstone caldera rim

Looking south over Lower Geyser Basin (foreground), Midway Geyser Basin, and Upper Geyser Basin, with the Red Mountains in the distance.

How a Caldera Forms

Stage One:
Magma rising from the interior of the earth forms a bulge and cracks on the surface.

Stage Two:
Pressure builds up and is released through the cracks in the form of hot gases, ash, and lava. Wind carries volcanic ash and deposits it on the landscape.

Stage Three:
The bulge sinks as the magma chamber collapses.

Stage Four:
The caldera takes on a dome shape as the magma continues to rise. Rhyolite flows out of the cracks.

The Annie, the first boat launched on Yellowstone Lake, 1871. The lake was created by glaciers.

Glaciers

Yellowstone is a land of fire and ice. Much of the scenery we enjoy in Yellowstone was shaped over thousands of years by sheets of ice called **glaciers.** The glaciers carved, gouged, and smoothed the Yellowstone landscape into the valleys, canyons, meadows, rivers, mountain peaks, and lakes we see today. Since the volcanoes last erupted, glaciers have covered the Yellowstone region at least ten times. Some of the glaciers were so thick that only the tops of the mountains poked out above the sheets of ice. Ice covered the top of **Mt. Washburn** during the most recent period of glaciation.

Rivers of Ice

Glaciers are rivers of ice. They form when more snow falls in the winter than melts in the spring and summer. Over thousands of years, the snow grows deeper and deeper. Year after year, as more snow piles on top, the snow below changes to ice due to the weight of the snowpack above.

When the ice is about 200 feet thick it begins to move downhill, like a slowly flowing river, and a glacier is born!

SLOW-MOVING GLACIER

Accumulation zone
(ice and snow accumulate)

Tributary glacier

Ablation zone
(ice is lost through melting and evaporation)

Terminus
(the end of the glacier)

Valley glacier

Terminal moraine
(glacial deposits of earth and stone)

Parts of a Glacier

GREASY WHEN WET

The weight of the ice in the glacier's center forces the edges to move. Yellowstone's glaciers slid on a thin layer of water at the bottom of the glacier. This water "greased" the glacier's slide over the rock underneath.

Yellowstone has had several periods of glaciation. One began around 300,000 years ago. The last period, called the Pinedale Glaciation, began 80,000 years ago, lasted 66,000 years, and ended 14,000 years ago. During that time, the glaciers covering Yellowstone were about 4,000 feet thick.

Full Speed Ahead!

As a glacier moves it **picks up boulders and rocks.** The glaciers slowly grind some of them into gravel and sand. Other rocks get a free ride in the ice, sometimes being carried miles before being dropped. **Glacial Boulder** near **Canyon Village** is the size of a small house. A glacier carried this big boulder more than 20 miles before leaving it behind.

The heavy glaciers scrape mountainsides clear as they bulldoze their path. The glaciers **carve valleys and canyons.** They create rivers and lakes. They leave behind rounded hills.

The glacier stops, melts, and retreats when the climate warms. Usually at the glacier's final front there will be a **moraine,** a hill made of the rocky debris bulldozed and left behind by the disappearing glacier.

Yellowstone's last glaciation ended around 14,000 years ago when the Pinedale glaciers melted and uncovered Yellowstone. Plants established themselves as the glaciers retreated. Meadows blossomed and forests grew. Deer, elk, bison, moose, bighorn sheep, bears, and wolves returned. Eagles and osprey once again fished in ice-free rivers and streams.

When the temperature was warm enough, Native Americans began visiting Yellowstone and using the area's many resources.

A glacier deposited this boulder in Pleasant Valley near Tower, 1890.

Bison graze near Soda Butte Creek in a valley carved by glaciers.

Native Americans and Explorers

Yellowstone's First Tourists

No one knows who Yellowstone's first visitors were. **Archaeologists,** scientists who study people of long ago, tell us that **Native Americans** were in Yellowstone 11,000 years ago. This was about 3,000 years after the glaciers began melting and retreating, uncovering Yellowstone's natural wonders and resources. Archaeologists have found more than 1,100 places in Yellowstone where Native Americans left evidence of their visits.

For thousands of years, Native Americans traveled through the Yellowstone region on their way to their summer hunting grounds and winter homes. They must have paused to marvel at Yellowstone's many unusual sights. Around 500 years ago, some Native Americans began making Yellowstone their home for the summer. **Crow, Nez Perce, Shoshone, Flathead, Blackfeet,** and **Bannock** tribes hunted buffalo, elk, bighorn sheep, and deer in and around Yellowstone. These native peoples left Yellowstone when the deep winter snows fell and game was hard to hunt.

The **Sheepeaters,** a small band of Shoshone Indians, liked Yellowstone so much they stayed year-round. A 19th-century fur trapper described the Sheepeaters as "well armed with bows and arrows pointed with obsidian," and "neatly clothed in dressed deer and sheepskins of the best quality."

SLOW 🏃 **WATCH FOR TOURISTS**

Obsidian points

Sheepeater family

Obsidian Fun Facts

The Native Americans came for food, water, and shelter. Then they discovered a cliff made of **obsidian**. Obsidian is a glassy volcanic rock. The obsidian was a treasure for the Native Americans. Obsidian can be chipped into razor-sharp pieces ideal for **arrowheads, knives, scrapers, spearpoints, and other tools.**

Obsidian arrowheads that are **11,000** years old have been discovered near **Yellowstone National Park.**

In the summers, the Sheepeaters lived in high mountain valleys and meadows. They hunted, fished, and gathered roots and berries. The bighorn sheep was the Sheepeaters' favorite game. They feasted on the meat and used the sheepskins for clothes. After heating the sheep's big horns in hot springs and straightening them, they bound two horns together to make powerful bows. A well-aimed arrow from a Sheepeater bow could go through a buffalo!

The Sheepeaters no longer live in Yellowstone. But their memory lives on in Yellowstone names: Sheepeater Cliffs, Sheepeater Canyon, Sheepeater Trail, and Shoshone Lake.

Bighorn sheep

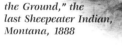

"Woman Under the Ground," the last Sheepeater Indian, Montana, 1888

Obsidian Cliff: A Mountain of Glass

Obsidian Cliff is one of the largest obsidian deposits in America. This towering mountain of glass rises more than 250 feet. Obsidian Cliff was formed around 180,000 years ago when a volcano erupted. The lava from the volcano cooled so fast that rock crystals didn't have time to form. The lava turned into a natural glass called **obsidian**.

Obsidian Cliff is so hard that 20th-century road builders in Yellowstone couldn't break the rocks with dynamite. They built fires at the base of the cliff, heated the obsidian, and splashed water onto it. The rapid cooling shattered the obsidian so the road could be finished! Of course, practices like these—destroying natural resources or collecting obsidian or any other natural object—are no longer permitted.

Midnight Black

Obsidian is usually midnight black. Some Yellowstone obsidian has streaks of yellow and red mixed with the black.

Yellowstone's Native Americans made their own tools from this unique obsidian. They also traded pieces of obsidian and tools they made with other tribes. Arrowheads chipped from Yellowstone obsidian have been found in Native American burial sites in Ohio!

Obsidian Cliff, 1884

New Explorers Arrive

Non-Indian visitors to what they called "the Yellowstone country" began to arrive in the early 1800s. In 1872, the U.S. government set aside part of the area as the first national park in the country and in the world—Yellowstone National Park.

John Colter Visits Yellowstone

John Colter—explorer, hunter, and trapper—is believed to have been the first white man to have seen Yellowstone's marvels.

He came west with the Lewis and Clark Expedition in 1804. A fearless, skilled woodsman, John Colter lived his life for adventure. Colter enjoyed the wide open wilderness so much that, instead of returning to St. Louis with Lewis and Clark in 1806, he turned back up the Missouri to trap beaver. During the winter of 1807-1808, Colter traveled 600 miles alone over frozen rivers and snow-covered mountains. One day he came to a **land of wonders.** He was astonished by skyrocketing geysers, hissing hot springs, and pots of bubbling mud. When John Colter told others what he had seen, *no one believed him!*

LAND OF WONDERS

"Grand Canyon of the Yellowstone," 1872

Exploring and Mapping

Not long after Colter visited Yellowstone, other **mountain men** came to the area to trap beaver. The valuable beaver furs were sold to make hats in Europe. These men told such fantastic tales about Yellowstone that other explorers wanted to see Yellowstone's wonders for themselves.

In May 1860, a large expedition tried to reach Yellowstone, but late-spring snowstorms ended their efforts. In 1869, a group from Montana explored Yellowstone. The next summer another expedition led by **General Henry Washburn** roamed through Yellowstone. Its members took measurements, made maps, and recorded Yellowstone's natural wonders. **Mt. Washburn,** one of Yellowstone National Park's best viewpoints, is named for the explorer.

↑ *"Castle Geyser," 1874*

← *The Hayden Expedition made this odometer to measure distances as they explored the area.*

↓ *"Valley of the Yellowstone," 1871*

Washburn Expedition map, 1870

Thomas Moran

William Henry Jackson

Hayden Expedition members, Dr. Ferdinand V. Hayden seated at center, 1870

An Amazing Idea!

Henry Washburn and his companions were greatly impressed by Yellowstone. Legend has it that, one night around the campfire, someone suggested that no one be allowed to claim land in Yellowstone. Washburn proposed that Yellowstone be set aside and protected as a special park for the entire nation, a national park.

In 1871, the United States Congress funded an expedition led by Dr. Ferdinand V. Hayden. Thomas Moran, an artist, and William Henry Jackson, a photographer, created images of Yellowstone's wildness. Dr. Hayden and his crew surveyed and mapped much of Yellowstone. Dr. Hayden's report, combined with Moran's stunning paintings and Jackson's striking black-and-white photographs, convinced Congress to pass a law protecting and preserving Yellowstone. On March 1, 1872, President U.S. Grant signed the law that created Yellowstone National Park.

 *"The First Official Exploration of the Yellowstone, Wyoming Region,"
1935. Shown are members of the Hayden Expedition.*

Yellowstone was "dedicated and set aside as a public park or pleasuring ground for the benefit and enjoyment of the people."

Yellowstone became our first national park and the first national park in the world.

...FOR THE BENEFIT AND ENJOYMENT OF THE PEOPLE. YUP. THAT WAS ME.

← *President Ulysses S. Grant*

↓ *U.S. Congressional Act, 1872*

March 1, 1872. CHAP. XXIV. — *An Act to set apart a certain Tract of Land lying near the ___ of the Yellowstone River as a public Park.*

Be it enacted by the Senate and House of Representatives of ___ States of America in Congress assembled, That the tract of l___ Territories of Montana and Wyoming, lying near the head___ the Yellowstone river, and described as follows, to wit, commen___ junction of Gardiner's river with the Yellowstone river, and r___ to the meridian passing ten miles to the eastward of the most ea___ of Yellowstone lake ; thence south along said meridian to the ___ latitude passing ten miles south of the most southern point of Y___ lake ; thence west along said parallel to the meridian passing ___ west of the most western point of Madison lake ; thence north___ meridian to the latitude of the junction of the Yellowstone and ___ rivers ; thence east to the place of beginning. is hereby reserve___ drawn from settlement, occupancy, or sale under the laws of ___ States, and dedicated and set apart as a public park or pleasu___ for the benefit and enjoyment of the people ; and all perso___ locate or settle upon or occupy the same, or any part there___ hereinafter provided, shall be considered trespassers and re___ from.

Public park established near the head-waters of the Yellowstone River. boundaries.

Certain persons locating, &c., thereon, to be trespassers.

Secretary of the Interior to

SEC. 2. That said public park shall be under the exclusi___ the Secretary of the Interior, whose duty it shall be, as so___

"FOR THE BENEFIT AND ENJOYMENT OF THE PEOPLE"

Roosevelt Arch

CAUTION
TALL TALES
DON'T BELIEVE ALL YOU HEAR

Tall Tales

When Yellowstone's first explorers returned with tales of water shooting hundreds of feet into the air and boiling pools hot enough to cook eggs, most people thought they were exaggerating Yellowstone's natural wonders.

Many early **explorers** and **mountain men** were skilled **storytellers.** They entertained their friends with tall tales told around campfires during long winter nights.

One mountain man's tale of hunting in Yellowstone's **petrified forests** went like this:

"I've trapped beaver and hunted on the Platte and Arkansas rivers, and way up on the Missouri and the Yaller Stone. But the hardest hunting I ever did was in the petrified forest. It was February when I come upon this forest in a Yellowstone valley with grass and trees as green as a summer day. I was plumb hungry so I shot a gobbling turkey bird out of tree.

"Well, that turkey's head rolled right to my feet and it was still a gobbling away. I picked up that turkey's head and just about started gobbling myself...it was made of stone! The bird was petrified!

"I looked close at the tree. It was stone, too! The grass and sagebrush were all rock solid. In fact, the whole darned valley was petrified right down to the sunbeams!

"I was so hungry I just broke off one of those sunbeams and roasted my turkey over it. That old bird was a bit tough but it filled me up so my stomach was as hard as a rock."

Yellowstone Thermal Features

Yellowstone National Park has more than 10,000 thermal features—more than all of the rest of the world combined. These thermal features include Yellowstone's famous **skyrocketing geysers, colorful hot springs, bubbling mud pots,** and **hissing fumaroles.** Three things create Yellowstone's thermal features: heat, water, and a "plumbing system."

Danger, Hot Water!

Yellowstone's many thermal features are beautiful but deadly. The water in the geysers and hot springs can be **above boiling** (199 degrees Fahrenheit, 92.8 degrees Celsius)! The crust around many thermal features is often eggshell thin and breaks very easily. Under the thin rock there is often scalding water.

For safety, Park rangers insist that visitors **stay on the boardwalks.** Hikers must also stick to the trails. Going off the boardwalk or trail in a thermal area is not only extremely dangerous—it also is against the law!

When It's Hot, It's Hot!

The heat source for the thermal features is the huge chamber of **magma** deep beneath Yellowstone's surface. Magma is melted rock from inside the earth, which has gathered in a deep chamber.

The magma heats the rocks around it. Then they are ready to heat seeping water to more than 400 degrees Fahrenheit, 204.4 degrees Celsius.

Great Fountain Geyser

DANGER
HOT H_2O

Call the Plumber!

Yellowstone's water comes from **rain** (average 15.1 inches per year) and **snow** (average 72.1 inches per year). Rainwater and melted snow seep down through Yellowstone's rocks. When the water reaches the hot rocks beneath Yellowstone's surface, the water begins to **heat**.

The hot water rises up through a web of cracks in the rocks. This has been nicknamed **"the plumbing system."** Some water shoots straight through the plumbing system to the surface. Sometimes, however, the water is blocked for a while. Either way, when the hot water finally escapes, it creates one of Yellowstone's many thermal features.

Scientists have calculated that the water fueling these thermal features is hundreds of years old. This is because it takes a long time for the rain and meltwater to seep deep into the earth.

Earthquakes, Nature's Plumber

As the boiling water perks upward, it dissolves **silica** (a white or colorless crystal like quartz) and other minerals. When the water cools, it deposits the minerals on the walls of the plumbing system. Sometimes these deposits "clog" the plumbing system and make it difficult for water to pass through.

Yellowstone experiences hundreds of small **earthquakes** each year. These earthquakes shake up the plumbing system, break up the silica deposits, and open new cracks. The frequent earthquakes keep Yellowstone's plumbing system in working condition. Sometimes, however, the earthquakes turn off one geyser and turn on another. In addition to local earthquakes, earthquakes as far away as Alaska can impact Yellowstone's thermal features! In 2002, an earthquake in Alaska caused more than 1,000 small earthquakes in Yellowstone. The earthquakes affected a few geysers in the Upper Geyser Basin, including **Daisy, Castle,** and **Plume.**

Geysers

A **geyser** is an unusual thermal feature that periodically erupts with showers of water and steam. The name geyser comes from Iceland's famous geyser named "Geysir." This "geyser" was named "geysir" or "gusher" in 1294 by an English monk touring Iceland. And geysers do gush!

Yellowstone has more than 300 active geysers, more than half of the total number on earth. What makes Yellowstone's geysers erupt? **Heat, water,** and **plugged-up plumbing!**

When hot water rising quickly in a geyser's plumbing system reaches a clog in its rocky

SMELLY AREA AHEAD

PU

What's that SMELL?

Some of Yellowstone thermal features smell like **rotten eggs.** The cause of the smell is **sulfuric acid** in the steam. As the sulfur goes into the air, it deposits yellow sulfur crystals on the rocks. If you smell rotten eggs, look for the telltale yellow sulfur!

Thermal Features Facts

Best known geyser:
Old Faithful
(average 130 feet)

Tallest geyser:
Steamboat
(400 feet)

Tallest predictable geyser:
Grand Geyser (200 feet)

Largest hot spring:
Grand Prismatic Spring
(375 feet across)

Cliff Geyser

pipes, the water is forced to slow down. The trapped water grows hotter and hotter until it becomes superheated and explodes into steam. The steam erupts as the geyser shoots water and steam into the air. The geyser continues erupting until it uses all of its water and the pressure drops.

The more water there is, the more explosive the eruption.

In the winter, Yellowstone's intense cold makes the eruptions even more dramatic when the hot steam condenses in the freezing air.

As the geyser settles down, more water enters the clogged pipes, is heated, flashes into steam, and erupts again. This pattern continues more or less on a regular basis.

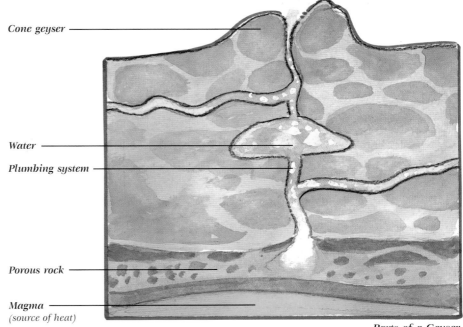

Cone geyser

Water

Plumbing system

Porous rock

Magma
(source of heat)

Parts of a Geyser

Castle Geyser

Thar' She Blows!

Park rangers are often able to predict how frequently a geyser will erupt. The intervals between geyser eruptions can vary wildly!

Old Faithful gets its name from the regularity of its eruptions (usually about every 90 minutes). **White Dome Geyser** erupts almost every 15 minutes. **Riverside Geyser** erupts every 6 to 7 hours. **Steamboat Geyser**, the largest in the world, may not erupt for years. Its last recorded eruption was on April 27, 2003. But when Steamboat does erupt, it is spectacular! For 10 minutes, Steamboat shoots its stream of steam and water 300 to 400 feet into the air. **Excelsior Geyser** hasn't erupted for more than 120 years!

Geysers usually announce their eruptions with a grumbling, rumbling sound before steam and water shoot into the air. Some geysers interact with one another. **Grand Geyser** and **Turban Geyser** are good examples. Grand Geyser erupts every 8 to 12 hours. A minute or two before Grand's eruption, nearby Turban Geyser erupts. The two geysers apparently share parts of the same plumbing system and water supply.

Hot Springs

Like a geyser, a **hot spring** is formed by water heated below the earth's surface. A hot spring is created where hot water can rise easily through cracks and fractures. A hot spring's **plumbing system isn't clogged** by mineral deposits. In the winter, clouds of condensing steam create ghostly shapes that swirl over the hot springs.

Hot springs bubble and steam. **Grand Prismatic Spring** in the **Midway Geyser Basin** is Yellowstone's largest hot spring. This deep-blue pool has rings of orange and yellow bacteria growing at its edge and in its runoff channels, which give Grand Prismatic its prism-like colors.

Morning Glory Pool near Old Faithful is another beautiful hot spring. Unfortunately, Morning Glory has lost some of its glory because careless folks have dropped litter into the hot spring. This has begun blocking the water flow. The hot water has cooled so much that algae grows, changing Morning Glory's deep-blue color.

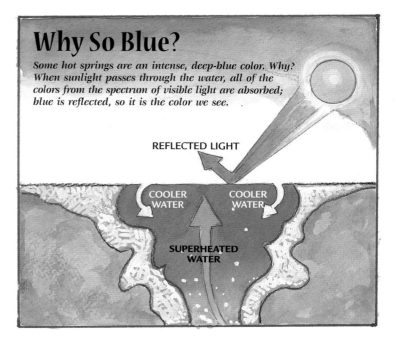

Why So Blue?

Some hot springs are an intense, deep-blue color. Why? When sunlight passes through the water, all of the colors from the spectrum of visible light are absorbed; blue is reflected, so it is the color we see.

REFLECTED LIGHT

COOLER WATER **COOLER WATER**

SUPERHEATED WATER

Debris removed from Morning Glory Pool in 1951 cleanup

PLEASE LEAVE NO TRACE

Morning Glory Pool

Grand Prismatic Spring

Living in a Hot Spring

Many of Yellowstone's hot springs would scald you if you dipped your finger into them. However, many tiny organisms, called **thermophiles**, call these hot springs home. Thermophiles thrive in water too hot for other life forms to survive.

Thermophiles color the hot springs and the rocks around them. Yellow and orange thermophiles like hotter water. Green and brown thermophiles are found in cooler water. Few thermophiles can live in the boiling water right where it enters the pool.

Some hot springs have mats of algae and bacteria at their edges. These mats range from yellow to orange to green, depending on the spring's heat.

Some hot springs are filled with clear, blue water. The beautiful blue color is created by water that is almost boiling and has few thermophiles.

NO LITTERING UP TO $100 FINE

Paint Pots & Bubbling Mud

Paint pots (or mud volcanoes, mud pots) are scattered throughout Yellowstone. One excellent collection is at **Artists' Paint Pots** in the **Gibbon Geyser Basin.** The mud in these paint pots is beige, gray, and pink. Acid in the hot water breaks down the rock in the basin and makes a white mud. The other colors are created when iron oxides tint the white mud.

These mud volcanoes are just another kind of hot spring. Steam and gas, rising in the springs, bubbles up through the mud. The mud-covered bubbles grow until they pop. Many Park visitors enjoy watching and hearing the boiling mud bubbles pop and plop.

In the fall, winter, and spring, the "paint" in these pots is thin and soupy from increased rain and snow. In late summer, however, when Yellowstone is drier, the mud thickens and the bubbles grow bigger.

Some mud volcanoes erupt with mud bubbles fifteen feet tall! Other mud pots sometimes spray mud out 25 feet.

Fuming Fumaroles

Fumaroles are called "dry geysers" because the underground water in a fumarole does not reach the surface. Fumaroles release steam and other gases. These steam vents sizzle, hiss, and roar as the steam rumbles through a fumarole's plumbing pipes.

At **Roaring Mountain,** you can enjoy watching fumaroles fume.

Fumaroles, Lower Geyser Basin

Yellowstone Landmarks

Old Faithful Geyser

Old Faithful Geyser is the most famous geyser in the world. Old Faithful is not the tallest geyser in the world, however. It is not the biggest geyser in the world either. But Old Faithful is famous because its eruptions can usually be predicted and it is easy to get to. In 1870 members of the famous Washburn Expedition called this geyser Old Faithful because of the regularity of its eruptions.

Like all geysers, Old Faithful relies on intense heat, water, and its own unique plumbing system. Old Faithful usually erupts about every 90 minutes—but don't count on it! Old Faithful is still on its own schedule, and eruptions can't be predicted exactly. Old Faithful

Old Faithful Facts

Height:
varies from 106 to 184 feet

Duration of eruption:
1.5 to 5 minutes

Intervals between eruptions:
45 to 120 minutes

Clogs in the plumbing:
one at 22 feet, one at 70 feet

Amount of water in each eruption:
3,700 to 8,400 gallons
of boiling water

MORE INFO

Old Faithful

erupts with relative regularity because it receives a steady flow of hot water through its underground plumbing system. Also, the geyser doesn't share its water and plumbing system with any other geysers.

In 1870, Old Faithful erupted every 60 to 65 minutes. In 1990, it erupted every 78 minutes. In 2001, Old Faithful showed off every 88 minutes. The park rangers use a formula to calculate when Old Faithful will next erupt. Their calculations are based on the time of Old Faithful's last eruption and how long it lasted.

So far, Old Faithful's eruptions have been recorded more than 137,000 times!

No matter what its internal schedule is, Old Faithful performs for thousands of tourists from around the world, day and night. Even when no one is there to watch, Old Faithful faithfully erupts.

Old Faithful announces its eruptions with some rumbling and small bursts of steam. Then a spurt of water shoots into the air, followed by a big burst of steam and water that climbs up to about 80 feet. Old Faithful's eruptions usually last from about two to five minutes.

Eruptions in winter are especially awesome, when Old Faithful's steam condenses spectacularly in the chilly air. Hardy visitors share Old Faithful's beauty with frost-covered bison enjoying the warmth of the geyser basin.

Would You Like a Cone?

Yellowstone has two distinct types of geysers: **cone** and **fountain**. Both are formed from silica deposited by hot water. This silica deposit creates a rock called **geyserite**.

A cone geyser, like Old Faithful, rises above the surface in a cone shape. Each geyser cone is distinctive, however. **Grotto Geyser** is one of Yellowstone's most unusual cone geysers. Scientists think that its early eruptions covered some nearby trees. They bent beneath the geyserite's weight, creating the "Swiss cheese" holes. **Castle Geyser** reminded early explorers of a castle. Cone geysers blast water into the air as if squirting it from a fire hose.

Fountain geysers form in basins that can hold pools of water. These geysers erupt through the pools before shooting water and steam into the air. **Grand Geyser** and **Echinus Geyser** are excellent examples of fountain geysers.

Grotto Geyser

Mammoth Hot Springs: Frozen Waterfalls of Rock

Minerva Terrace

Mammoth Hot Springs is quite different from most of Yellowstone's hot springs. Some folks have called these springs a "mountain turning itself inside out." Others marvel at these unusual springs, calling them a "frozen waterfall."

No matter the name, Mammoth Hot Springs is not the same as Yellowstone's other hot springs.

Mammoth Hot Springs is formed by hot water rising through a plumbing system just like those of the Park's other hot springs. At Mammoth, the rocks make the difference. Instead of perking up through volcanic rocks, Mammoth's hot water rises through an ancient bed of limestone. This **limestone** was laid down millions of years ago when a sea covered the Yellowstone region.

The hot water rising through the cracks in the limestone is actually dissolving the rock. Water carries this dissolved limestone upward until it reaches the surface. As the water spills out of the springs and cools, it deposits the dissolved limestone onto a series of **terraces.** These give Mammoth Hot Springs its "frozen waterfall" appearance.

This new rock is called **travertine.** The amount of water, the temperature of the water, earthquakes, and blocked underground plumbing affect the amount of travertine formed in any one area.

At Mammoth Hot Springs, you can see geology in action. An average of eight inches of new travertine is deposited each year in some of the most active areas. In several spots almost two feet of new rock is formed every year! At **Opal Terrace,** the deposits are growing so fast that they threaten to overwhelm the nearby Executive House.

Mammoth Hot Springs is very colorful. The newest terraces are brown, green, yellow, pink, and orange. Older terraces are white, and the oldest terraces are gray. These colors come from the bacteria and algae that thrive in these hot springs.

Like all of Yellowstone's thermal features, Mammoth Hot Springs needs a source of heat. Although it is a mile from most of Yellowstone's other hot spots, Mammoth also gets its heat from the magma below. All year long, the water in the hot springs is about 170 degrees Fahrenheit (76.7 degrees Celsius).

KEEP OFF THE TRAVERTINE

INSIDE OUT

It is estimated that nearly one million gallons of hot water bubble out of **Mammoth Hot Springs** every day. The water flowing from Mammoth Hot Springs fell as rain or snow many years ago. It takes a long time for the water to seep down and come back up with its load of dissolved limestone. Thousands of pounds of new travertine are left behind each day as this water flows away. Because the travertine is formed from the rocks below the hot springs, people called Mammoth a "mountain turning itself inside out."

Elk Lawn Mowers

Mammoth Hot Springs is an excellent place to see **elk**. When the U.S. Cavalry was stationed at **Fort Yellowstone** (then located here), they built a parade ground seeded with grass and clover. This is the only lawn in Yellowstone National Park.

No one needs to mow this lawn, however. A resident herd of elk keeps the grass "cut" all summer! In winter, the elk like to warm themselves on the hot spring terraces.

Elk are sometimes called by their Shawnee Indian name **wapiti**. Like most of Yellowstone's animals, wapiti are not tame. Visitors are warned not to get any closer than 25 yards (75 feet, almost as far as it is from home plate to first base in baseball) to elk anywhere in the Park.

The lawns of Mammoth are also home to dozens of **Uintah ground squirrels**. These squirrels burrow underground where they spend the seven coldest months of the year. In summer, busy ground squirrels seem to be everywhere, gathering food and staring at tourists! Uintah ground squirrels scamper throughout Yellowstone.

Elk cow and calf

Hats Off

One of Mammoth's most unusual features is **Liberty Cap**. This 37-foot-tall cone was once a hot spring. Unlike Yellowstone's other cones—which were formed by geysers—Liberty Cap is made of travertine deposited by a hot spring.

Geologists estimate that Liberty Cap is more than 2,500 years old. Liberty Cap is believed to be extinct, because it has been inactive since 1871.

Nearby, you will find **Devil's Thumb**, another extinct cone.

Liberty Cap

Fort Yellowstone, 1916

Yellowstone Lake Fun Facts

North America's highest lake:
7,732 feet above sea level.

Largest mountain lake in
the United States
14 miles wide
20 miles long
110 miles of shoreline
136 square miles
Average depth: 139 feet
Deepest spot: 439 feet
125 streams feed Yellowstone Lake

Islands:
Pelican Roost, Carrington, Sandy,
Rocky, Peale, Dot, Stevenson, Frank

Underwater Hot Spot: 212 degrees
Fahrenheit (100 degrees Celsius),
in Mary Bay

Average summer temperature:
45 degrees Fahrenheit
(7.2 degrees Celsius)

Lake bottom:
42 degrees Fahrenheit all year
(5.6 degrees Celsius)

Swimming is allowed in Yellowstone
Lake but not suggested because the
lake is *so cold!*

Yellowstone Lake and River

Yellowstone National Park was created by volcanic fire and shaped by glacial ice. Both fire and ice helped form **Yellowstone Lake,** one of Yellowstone's gems.

The **volcanic blast** of the Lava Creek explosion 640,000 years ago created the Yellowstone caldera and the basin for Yellowstone Lake. About 14,000 years ago, when the last **glaciers** melted, the basin filled with ice-cold water—and Yellowstone Lake was born.

One of the largest geyser basins in the Park is the **West Thumb Basin** on the shores of Yellowstone Lake. Here geysers erupt, hot springs boil, and mud pots bubble.

The famous **Fishing Cone** is here, too. Indians, explorers, and even early-day tourists once stood on Fishing Cone, caught cutthroat trout, and cooked them (still on the hook) in Fishing Cone's boiling water. *(This is no longer allowed!)*

More than 100 streams replenish Yellowstone Lake. One of these streams is the headwaters of the **Yellowstone River,** which enters the lake on the south shore. The river leaves Yellowstone Lake at **Fishing Bridge** and meanders north through lush meadows and evergreen forests. All at once, however, the calm Yellowstone River is transformed into a rushing, roaring river.

John Muir, one of America's first naturalists, wrote about this change:

"Then suddenly, as if preparing for hard work, it [the river] *rushes eagerly forward rejoicing in its strength, breaks into foam-bloom, and goes thundering down into the Grand Canyon in two magnificent falls, one hundred and three hundred feet high."*

Fishing Cone, 1895

Look Out Below!

The river first plunges 109 feet over **Upper Falls**. Here the river has carved a gap in the volcanic rock. **Uncle Tom's Overlook** is an excellent place to view Upper Falls.

The river rushes on to **Lower Falls**, where it tumbles 308 feet before crashing to the river bed below. The views of the misty, rainbow-making Lower Falls have inspired artists from painter Thomas Moran in 1871 to today. The best place to view the Lower Falls is from either **Artist Point** or **Inspiration Point**.

Upper Falls of the Yellowstone

BE CAREFUL
WATCH YOUR STEP

Lower Falls

What's in a Name?

The **Hidatsa Indians** named the **Yellowstone River**. They called it "Mi Tsi A-Da-Zi" for the yellow sandstone cliffs along the river in Montana. "Mi Tsi A-Da-Zi" means "Rock Yellow River." Most likely, these native people never saw the **Grand Canyon of the Yellowstone River**. They visited the river at its other end, where it flows into the Missouri River, in today's northeastern Montana.

The **French fur trappers and traders** called it "Roche Jaune" or "Yellow Rock River." **English-speaking trappers and explorers** called it the Yellowstone River.

Grand Canyon of the Yellowstone River

Grand Canyon of the Yellowstone River

Yellowstone's volcanic past comes to light at the falls. Here the Yellowstone River begins carving the magnificent **Grand Canyon of the Yellowstone** through thousands of feet of **volcanic rhyolite.** The canyon walls seem to have been painted with dozens of colors: black, off-white, yellow, orange, red, pink, green, and brown. The palette of colors comes from the natural color of the rocks themselves, weathering, steam, hot water, and plants. One early travel writer noted, "The whole gorge flames. It is as though rainbows had fallen out of the sky and hung themselves there like glorious banners."

Yellowstone's yellow stones are obvious in the canyon. Hot water and steam perking through the rhyolite have created the various shades of yellow, orange, red, and pink. The black is made either by the naturally black mineral magnetite or by lichens, plants that grow on the rocks. Algae, moss, and trees make the green.

Grand Canyon Fun Facts

Length: 20 miles from the Upper Falls to Tower Junction

Width: 1,500-4,000 feet

Depth: 800-1,200 feet

Lower Falls height: 308 feet

Upper Falls height: 109 feet

Yellowstone Wildlife

These people are too close to the bison.

CAUTION
WILD ANIMALS ARE
UNPREDICTABLE
STAY BACK

Not a Zoo!

Some park visitors, when they see animals, think that Yellowstone is just one big zoo. It is not!

Each year Park visitors are injured when they get too close to Yellowstone's large mammals.

To help protect all visitors, park rangers give warnings about bears and where they are. You should come no closer than 100 yards (the length of a football field) to a bear.

Rangers also tell folks how much distance to keep between themselves and other animals, especially when taking pictures. The closest you should approach bison, elk, deer, moose, wolves, coyotes, and bighorn sheep is 25 yards (or 75 feet, almost as far as it is between home plate and first base in baseball). Yellowstone animals might appear to be tame, but they are wild, unpredictable, and dangerous.

Bison can weigh up to 2,000 pounds. They can sprint up to 30 miles an hour! That is much faster than the fastest human, including you!

Bald eagle

SPEED CHECKED BY RADAR

Eagles, Symbols of Success!

In 1989, the year after the fires scorched Yellowstone, only 3 baby **bald eagles** fledged. By 2003, there were 32 nesting pairs of bald eagles in the Park. This is the highest number ever recorded in Yellowstone. That year, 24 baby bald eagles survived and took to Yellowstone's skies.

More than half of Yellowstone's bald eagles live near **Yellowstone Lake.** The lake's crystal-clear waters, population of cutthroat trout, and towering trees entice the eagles to make this part of the park their summer home. The eagles dive from the trees to grab trout out of the lake for their dinner. In the winter, when the lake is frozen three feet thick, the eagles migrate.

Speeding Tickets

Pronghorn antelope: 61 mph
Elk: 45 mph
Coyote: 43 mph
Moose: 35 mph
White tailed Deer: 30 mph
Bison: 30 mph
Human: 15 mph
Squirrel: 12 mph
Snail: 0.03 mph

Osprey

Ospreys, The Fishing Hawks

Ospreys, or fish hawks, however, haven't done so well. In 2003, there were only 58 osprey nests. Just 17 young ospreys survived the summer.

In 1992, there had been 100 nesting pairs of ospreys in the Park. A bolt of lightning sparked a fire on Frank Island in 2003, once home to dozens of ospreys. This fire burned almost the entire island, destroying all but one osprey nest there.

Park rangers understand that Yellowstone is a land of changes. They believe that the ospreys will adapt to these changes and more ospreys will dive for fish in Yellowstone's rivers and lakes.

Return of the Wolf

"Ooo-oo-oooo!"

For thousands of years, the haunting howl of wild wolf packs echoed through Yellowstone. By 1925, settlers and trappers had killed all of the wolves outside the Park to protect sheep and cattle. By 1940, Yellowstone National Park managers eliminated wolves to protect certain wildlife species.

In 1973, **gray wolves** were added to the Federal Endangered Species List. In 1995 and 1996, 31 gray wolves from Canada were **reintroduced** into the Park. For more than 70 years, no wolves had howled, prowled, or played in Yellowstone. Some people are happy to see wolves back in the Park, and others are not. Wolves don't understand Park boundaries and some have wandered outside the Park onto private property, including ranches with livestock, which some wolves have preyed upon.

Gray wolf

Surprise!

Scientists have been surprised by many **unexpected consequences** of placing **wolves** back into Yellowstone's web of life.

Bears benefit from wolves. Bears chase wolves away from wolf kills to feast on the fresh meat themselves. For example, one grizzly bear chased away a pack of fifteen wolves so it could eat a bison the wolves had killed. With more food like this to eat, the Yellowstone's bear population is increasing.

Wolves help **fish,** too! How? The numerous elk in Yellowstone have over-grazed willow, cottonwood, and other plants. The elk population is reduced by the hungry wolves. The elk are also forced to move around more to avoid the wolves, allowing the plants to recover. These plants shade stream water and make it colder and better for trout.

John Muir said it best: *"When we try to pick out anything by itself, we find it hitched to everything else in the universe."*

Wolf pack

Wolf being released into acclimation pen

Turn on the Radio!

Scientists keep track of wolves roaming Yellowstone by turning on the radio. Biologists fit special **radio collars** around a wolf's neck and select a "station" or frequency for the wolf. These radio collars help scientists locate the dens where the wolves raise and feed their pups. Radio-collared wolves lead scientists to wolf kill-sites and to their rendezvous sites, where wolf pups hide while the adults hunt. Scientists identify dead wolves or wolves killing sheep and cattle by their radios.

Wolf or Coyote?

Wolves and **coyotes** are both in the dog family, *Canidae*. However, a coyote is much smaller than a wolf and weighs only about 30 pounds. A wolf weighs 80 to 130 pounds. Coyotes have slim bodies with pointed noses and long, bushy tails. They hunt rodents by stalking and then pouncing on them. Coyotes are abundant and are more common to see than wolves in Yellowstone.

Wolves are larger and broader than coyotes. They have long front legs. Their paw prints are the size of a human hand. Wolves are most active at dawn and dusk.

The best place to see a wolf in Yellowstone is in the **Lamar Valley** between **Tower** and **Cooke City**. This is where the largest wolf pack, the **Druid Peak Pack**, lives.

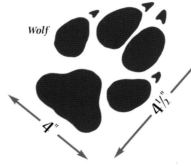
wolf

Coyote

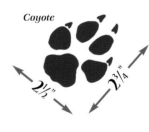

Wolf 4" 4½"

Coyote 2½" 2¾"

WOLF VS. COYOTE

	GRAY WOLVES (adult)	COYOTES (adult)
Length:	4 to 6 feet	3.6 to 4.4 feet
Height:	26 to 36 inches at the shoulder	16 to 20 inches at the shoulder
Weight:	80 to 130 pounds	25 to 35 pounds
Color:	buff tans grizzled with gray and black, but can also be black or white	gray or reddish brown with rusty legs, feet, and ears, and whitish throat and belly
Ears:	rounded, relatively short	pointed, relatively long
Muzzle:	large and blocky	petite and pointed

Coyotes

Bears

Yellowstone is home to two kinds of bears: grizzly bears and black bears.

Did I See a Grizzly Bear or a Black Bear?

There are big differences between grizzly bears and black bears.

But don't get close enough to check all of these characteristics! The law states that you must stay at least 100 yards (the length of a football field) away from any bear, grizzly or black.

Grizzly bear

	GRIZZLY (adult)	BLACK (adult)
Length:	6 to 7 feet	5 to 6 feet
Height:	3.5 feet at the shoulder	3 feet at the shoulder
Weight:	200 to 700 pounds	135 to 315 pounds
Color:	black to blonde, frequently with white-tipped fur and light-brown girth band	from pure black to brown, cinnamon, or blonde, some with a light-brown muzzle
Profile:	dish-shaped face	straight or flat face
Ears:	smaller, rounded	larger, pointed, more erect
Shoulder:	distinctive hump of muscle over shoulders	no hump
Other:	shoulder hump is highest point of the body	rump is highest point of the body

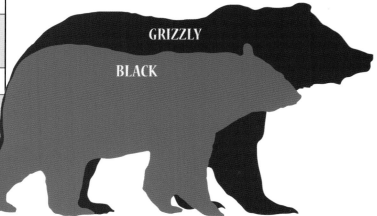

A Grizzly Tale

"The only good grizzly bear is a dead grizzly bear!" used to be a common saying in the Yellowstone region.

The grizzlies did die. Humans feared *Ursus arctos horribilis,* the grizzly bear. In 1970, only 200 grizzly bears still lived in the Yellowstone region.

In 1975, Grizzly bears were added to the Federal Endangered Species List as a "threatened species." This means their numbers were low but not low enough to be considered "endangered."

The grizzly bear population is now growing in Yellowstone. Between 300 and 600 grizzly bears inhabit the Yellowstone ecosystem. The ecosystem is 18 million acres and includes national forests around the Park. Grizzly bears hibernate each winter and come out in the spring between March and May.

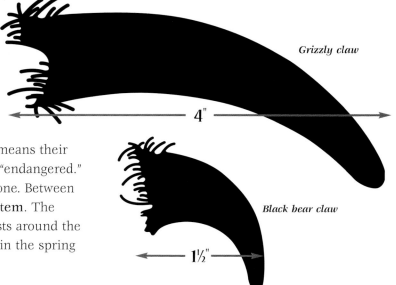

Grizzly claw

4"

Black bear claw

1½"

Omnivores

Bears are omnivores. They eat meat and plants. With their long, sharp, and curved claws they dig beetles, grubs, ants, and roots to eat. In the spring, the spawning cutthroat trout are important food for the hungry bears as they emerge from their dens.

In 1970, Yellowstone Park began to enforce strict rules about feeding bears, especially black bears. The goal of the rules was to keep human food out of the bears' paws. Often, if bears acquire a taste for human food, they will look for more tasty tidbits. This food is not healthy for the bears. Looking for it also leads to more bear–human encounters.

Before the 1970 rules were enacted, there were about 48 bear-related injuries to park visitors every year! Today the annual average is only one!

Bear Sense!

When hiking in **bear country** you should clap and make noise as you walk. You don't want to surprise a bear that might be sharing the same trail. **Never hike alone!** There is safety in numbers.

If you do meet a bear, don't run. Bears run fast! A bear can run 100 yards in six seconds. If you see a bear at a distance, the best thing to do is to drop your head and back away. Looking into the eyes of a bear challenges it. If the bear is very close, drop down to the ground and bring your knees to your stomach. Keep your backpack on as protection. Cover your neck with your arms.

Don't worry. Out of 125 million visitors to Yellowstone National Park, bears are responsible for only ten deaths.

Black bear

Something Fishy in Yellowstone: Cutthroat Trout

Yellowstone Lake and River have the largest **cutthroat trout** population in the world. But these special fish are in trouble.

Mackinaw lake trout were illegally introduced into **Yellowstone Lake.** With no natural predators, the trout are pushing out the cutthroat trout. One lake trout caught had 20 pounds of cutthroat trout inside its stomach!

Anglers catch about 4,000 lake trout each year to try to keep their numbers down. Because more than 40 species of animals in Yellowstone National Park depend on the cutthroat trout, the survival of the cutthroat trout is important. Scientists are putting **transmitters** on some cutthroat to monitor them.

Imagine how surprised the scientists were when they heard the beeping of a fish transmitter over their heads. Had they discovered a mysterious flying fish? No. One cutthroat the scientist had tagged had become a pelican's lunch!

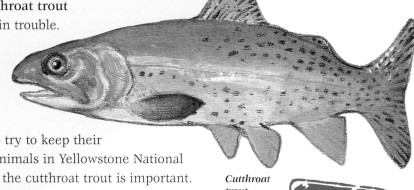

Cutthroat trout

Buffalo or a Bison?

Yellowstone National Park is home to a herd of about 4,000 **American bison,** commonly called **buffalo.** While it's okay to call them buffalo, these bison are not true buffalo. An example of a true buffalo is the water buffalo of India and southeast Asia.

The huge, shaggy bison have lived in Yellowstone since the last glaciers melted. They provided food, shelter, and clothing for many Native Americans as well early explorers in the area.

American bison

Millions of bison once roamed America's grasslands. Most of these majestic animals (more than 60 million) were slaughtered for their meat and hides during the 19th century. Around 100 years ago, it looked as if the bison, an American symbol, would become extinct. Through conservation efforts, however, the bison have recovered. Today more than 150,000 majestic bison live in public and private herds throughout Canada and the United States.

Yellowstone's bison herd is **America's last wild and free-ranging herd.** The bison population fluctuates according to food availability and the severity of winters. In the summer, the bison roam throughout the Park feeding on grasses and sedges. In the winter, they hang around the warm thermal areas. Some bison, however, migrate beyond the Park's protective borders, which causes conflicts with people to occur.

Bison: A Very Useful Animal

The region's Native American tribes tried to use every part of the animal.

Horns: spoons, cups, toys, powder horns

Bones: knives, shovels, winter sleds (ribs), war clubs

Hooves: glue, rattles

Skull: ceremonial object

Hair: rope

Hide: tipis, clothes, bedding, moccasins, dolls, quivers

Meat: food

Muscles: thread, bowstrings

Tail: flyswatter, tipi decorations

Dung: fire fuel

Bison grazing in Lower Geyser Basin

Pronghorn

Like the bison, millions of swift **pronghorns** (commonly called "antelopes") once lived in America's grasslands. Hunting drastically reduced their numbers. There are 200 to 500 pronghorns living in Yellowstone today. Pronghorns are best viewed in the summertime, especially in the **Lamar Valley** near the north entrance.

Antlers or Horn?

Is there a difference between **antlers** and **horns**? Yes! Animals like **mule deer, whitetailed deer, elk,** and **moose** grow a new set of antlers each spring. At first these antlers are covered with "velvet." Later, the animal scrapes the velvet off to uncover its hard new antlers. Each autumn, the antlers fall off. Older elk and deer have bigger antlers. Female deer, elk, and moose don't grow antlers.

Pronghorn

Bighorn sheep

Moose

ANTLERS | HORNS

Pronghorn

Moose

Pronghorns and **bighorn sheep** are animals with horns. Every year, bighorn sheep grow a new ring of bone-like material on their horns. Counting the number of rings on a sheep horn tells you how old the animal is.

Scientists can tell how old a deer or elk is by looking at its teeth. Each year elk and deer add a new hard layer to their teeth. The number of teeth rings reveals the animal's age.

Moose on the Loose

There are moose on the loose in Yellowstone. These large animals are usually glimpsed near ponds or wetlands. Moose are the largest antlered animals in Yellowstone.

A bull moose (male) weighs about 1,000 pounds; females weigh up to 900 pounds.

LOOSE MOOSE ZONE

Ever Herd (Heard) of Elk?

More than 35,000 **elk** roam the Yellowstone region in herds of different sizes. They can be seen eating in the meadows of the **Lamar Valley,** grazing in **Elk Park** southwest of Norris, or "mowing" the lawn at **Mammoth Hot Springs.** Elk prefer the high country in the summer and lowland valleys in the winter, but they can usually be spotted in many areas of the Park.

Elk

Elk are large mammals. Males can weigh around 700 pounds. Female elk weigh between 400 to 600 pounds. The fur of the males is lighter than that of the females. Males begin growing their antlers in the spring. By fall, when they are used for fighting, the antlers can be huge! The antlers fall off after winter so that new, bigger ones can grow.

Elk walk on their hooves. Their tracks look like two half moons facing each other. If you don't see an elk, maybe you can see the tracks where one walked.

Elk have white rear-ends. The Shawnee Indians called the elk **wapiti,** or white-rump. Visitors often see this white rear-end in a brushy area before seeing the rest of the elk.

Many elk are seen in the fall when the mating season begins. A wilderness thrill is to hear a male elk make his loud, high-pitched "bugle." An elk's bugle can he heard for miles, warning other elk to keep away or telling his female friends to gather round.

Hopefully, you'll have seen or heard a herd of Yellowstone's elk when you visit.

ELK AT WORK AHEAD

Feathered Fair-Weather Friends

Tanagers are brightly colored birds that travel to Yellowstone—where the food is abundant and there's plenty of space for nests—to raise their young. As winter approaches and food becomes scarce in Yellowstone, tanagers migrate to South America.

It's Official!

Official Yellowstone Park Flower: Western or Rocky Mountain fringed gentian

Trumpeter swan

Trumpeter Swans

Do you want to see a famous star in Yellowstone? Look for the snow-white, black-beaked **trumpeter swans** swimming in the **Yellowstone River** or paddling in Swan Lake. A trumpeter swan starred as the main character in *The Ugly Duckling.* Trumpeter swans also danced to fame in the ballet "Swan Lake."

These magnificent swans have long necks and swim very gracefully. Their distinctive *"koh-koh, koh-koh"* call while swimming is one to listen for and enjoy. When flying, trumpeter swans make the loud, **trumpet-like calls** for which they earned their name.

Trumpeter swans, one of three kinds of swans, are the largest water birds in North America. The wingspan of a male trumpeter swan can reach seven feet! Trumpeter swans are the world's heaviest flying birds. Adults weigh between 23 to 30 pounds. But they can fly more than 20 miles an hour to migrate or escape enemies. Trumpeter swans fight back with their long, strong wings when they are attacked.

Trumpeter swans bob their heads up and down and call to their companions when they feed. Their favorite places for nests are on the tops of muskrat lodges, where they can safely lay their eggs. Pairs of trumpeter swans mate for life.

These special birds almost became extinct at the end of the 1800s. Strong conservation efforts, like those practiced in Yellowstone, are giving these rare swans a chance to survive. Trumpeter swans are rugged, strong birds that can brave temperatures of 40 degrees below zero in the winter. Today, about 17 pairs of trumpeter swans spend the entire year in Yellowstone.

Is it a Bird? Is it a Plane?
It's a Sandhill Crane!

Before you see a **sandhill crane,** you might hear its unique *"garooo-a-a-a"* cry as it flies through the sky or feeds in a wetland or meadow.

Adult sandhill cranes are usually tall, gray birds with long legs and a long neck. They have a "cap" of red feathers on their heads. But the Yellowstone sandhill cranes sometimes look reddish brown. This is because they spread Yellowstone's red soil on their feathers while preening or cleaning them.

Sandhill cranes are found near the edge of aspen groves or near willows and lodgepole pines hunting for food or seeking protection. Sandhill cranes inhabit the **Fountain** and **Belcher Flats** parts of the Park in the summer. They migrate south in September when the days turn colder.

Like many visitors to Yellowstone, sandhill cranes spend their winters someplace else. Yellowstone's sandhill cranes usually

CAN YOU SAY GAROOO-A-A-A?

SOMEPLACE ELSE

Sandhill crane

are in Mexico and New Mexico in the winter before migrating back to Yellowstone in March or early April for the summer season. Flocks of more than 200 sandhill cranes can be seen winging their way to Yellowstone National Park.

Once in the Park, the cranes leave their flocks and live together in pairs. The four-foot-tall cranes build nests for their two eggs in wetland areas. They feed on insects, frogs, worms, and mice. And they **dance!**

Sandhill cranes dance a courtship dance. The birds take tall steps while raising their five-foot wings. One crane, then the other leap into the air. They bend their necks, turn their heads, and bow. If you see the sandhill cranes dance, you have seen one of nature's wonders!

Treetop Diner

Porcupines eat bark, buds, and leaves. Using their sharp, curved claws and strong muscles, they expertly climb into treetops to dine. Often they strip twigs of their bark and buds and discard the stems like a picked bone.

A Prickly Position

What Park animal weighs only about 22 pounds but can defend itself against a 300-pound bear? A porcupine! With 30,000 sharp quills, a porcupine can protect itself against almost any predator.

When threatened, a porcupine turns around and bats the attacker with its quill-filled tail. If the tail strikes the animal, the loosely held quills lodge into the attacker's body. These hollow quills expand once inside an animal's skin, and the barbs make them difficult and painful to remove.

If you spot a porcupine, leave it alone! You might see one lumbering along a Yellowstone path or waddling toward a tree. More likely, you will spot them draped over a branch or curled up in a ball in a tree. Porcupines tend to doze during the day and are more active at night. These rodents are solitary creatures living in rock crevices or tree holes in the winter; they do not hibernate.

Going to Bat For Bats

Does the thought of a **bat** bug you? It shouldn't! Bats eat the bugs that really do bug you! Yellowstone's bats feed on millions of bugs each year, especially pesky mosquitoes.

Yellowstone has four kinds of bats: **long-eared** (rare), **big-eared, big brown,** and **little brown.** Little brown bats can eat 600 mosquitoes in an hour. That's ten mosquitoes in a minute! That's more than you can slap! Without the help of bats, Yellowstone's many marvels wouldn't be nearly as much fun to enjoy.

Yellowstone's bats come out to eat when most visitors are getting ready for bed. As the sun sets, bats leave their roosts in caves, under bridges, and under

Long-eared bat

the eaves of historic buildings to feast on insects. Using their silent sonar, the bats dart and swoop through the evening sky gobbling up bugs. Besides mosquitoes, the bats eat moths, flies, beetles, and other insects.

Yellowstone's most common bat is the **little brown bat.** These bats are three to four inches long. They have furry bodies. Their wings, however, have no hair. Scientists sometimes capture a few of Yellowstone's bats to study them. The bats are then released to eat more bugs.

Bats are often feared by humans. However, these flying mammals are friendly neighbors. Like all animals in Yellowstone, bats are protected. Park rangers and staff go to bat for bats to make sure they are not injured and disturbed. If you see a bat flitting in the air at dusk in summer, thank it for helping eat those 600 mosquitoes an hour that might be biting you! If you are in Yellowstone in the winter, you won't see bats. They hide and hibernate for those six months.

Otters

Little brown bat

Underwater Buffet

Safely underwater, the otters zoom around and eat fish, frogs, turtles, and crayfish. Otters can swim underwater for two to three minutes and dive as deep at 35 feet.

You "Otter" Watch Out!

When you are near Yellowstone's rivers, streams, and lakes, keep an eye out for the playful **river otter.** The otters might be sliding down snowbanks into the water in the winter or diving in waterfalls in the summer. These animals always seem on the go, playing with each other or cleaning their thick protective fur. Otters must keep their fur coats in excellent condition in order to survive in icy water. If their coats become matted, otters can freeze to death.

River otters spend lots of time on land, which makes them easy for hungry eagles or coyotes to spot. Otters, however, rarely stray far from water. When danger comes, they slip and slide to safety. But otters have sharp teeth and they will fiercely fight a coyote trying to steal one of their fish dinners.

River otters build their homes in riverbanks or use abandoned muskrat or beaver lodges. Here, the litter of baby pups is born in the middle of winter. The pups live inside the lodge until spring, when they go out together as a family into the world. The pups stay with their moms for 18 months, learning to survive before setting out on their own in Yellowstone National Park.

Yellowstone On Fire!

Lightning Strikes!

On the afternoon of June 23, 1988, storm clouds rolled over parts of the park. Thunder rumbled. A **single bolt of lightning** zigzagged down, lighting a small **fire** on the southern side of Yellowstone. Two days later, another fire started in Yellowstone's western corner. Five days later, another natural fire began.

Yellowstone's managers knew each fire's location and its size. Instead of putting the fires out, they followed the Park's "let it burn" policy. In recent years, abnormally rainy summers had persisted; rain typically extinguished most natural fires. Because no life or property was threatened, these early fires were allowed to burn.

However, heat, high winds, no rain, and additional fires (one started by human carelessness) forced Park rangers to begin fighting the fires.

But it was almost too little, too late. Before anyone realized what was happening, fire swept toward **Grant Village.** Firefighters battled this fire to a standstill at the edge of the village complex of shops, hotels, and restaurants.

Another fire began burning toward historic **Old Faithful Inn** beside **Old Faithful geyser.** Many firefighters and employees alike worked hard to save this historic building.

How Dry I Am!

The summer of 1988 in Yellowstone had been exceptionally dry. During the winter before, Yellowstone had received very little snowfall. By late July, there was little moisture in the air, in the ground, and in the plants. Yellowstone and the surrounding region were in an extreme drought.

Live trees had less moisture than kiln-dried lumber that is used to build homes. Tens of thousands of lodgepole pines killed by bark beetles stood like brown matchsticks.

A Drop in the Bucket

Helicopters scooped thousands of gallons of water out of rivers and streams to drop on the fires. **Air tankers** dropped more water and fire-retardant chemicals on the advancing fires. **Fire engines** pumped water onto buildings to soak them. They put out sparks carried and dropped by the wind. **Firefighters** chopped firebreaks to halt the blazes. **Bulldozers** etched roads and fire lines primarily through national forests so firefighters and equipment could be moved to confront the fires. **Pack horses and mules** hauled firefighting equipment and food to firefighters in the distant back country.

At night, **planes** flew over Yellowstone taking pictures of the blazes so fire commanders would know where to send their crews the following day.

Clouds of smoke rose into the sky and drifted east. People hundreds, then thousands, of miles away smelled the smoke. Ash floated down from the sky more than 100 miles away from Yellowstone.

A military C-130 tanker drops a load of retardant on the North Fork Fire near West Yellowstone. A total of 1.4 million gallons of retardant were dropped on the Yellowstone fires.

Satellite image of 1988 Yellowstone fire smoke plumes

Break Out the Calculator!

What it took to fight the fires in and around Yellowstone:

$120 million
117 aircraft
100 fire engines
1.4 million gallons of flame retardant
25,000 firefighters
2 human lives
665 miles of fire line dug by hand
137 miles of fire lines scraped by bulldozers
40 cabins and homes burned

Map of the 1988 Yellowstone fires

Map labels:
HELLROARING FIRE
STORM CREEK FIRE
Gardiner
FAN FIRE
Mammoth
Tower-Roosevelt
NORTH FORK FIRE
Norris
Canyon Village
CLOVER MIST FIRE
West Yellowstone
Old Faithful
Grant Village
SNAKE RIVER COMPLEX
MINK CREEK FIRE
HUCK FIRE

Black Saturday

The worst was yet to come. On Saturday, August 19, Yellowstone seemed to explode in flames. Winds of 30 to 40 miles per hour whipped up the blaze. Some winds gusted with hurricane force of 70 miles per hour! Firefighting planes and helicopters were grounded because the winds were too strong.

Flames rocketed 200 feet in the air. Green trees exploded into fireballs.

On that one day, **Black Saturday,** the fires consumed 165,000 acres. On Black Saturday, Yellowstone's fires had **doubled in size,** burning five times as much of the Park as had been burned in the previous 16 years combined!

The Aftermath

On August 22, the **U.S. Army** was called in to help the exhausted firefighters. The war against the fires was waged into September, when **rain** and **snow** finally accomplished what humans could not. Nature had started most of the fires. Nature put them out.

Patchwork Quilt

Eight major fires burned in Yellowstone during the summer of 1988. By the time the fires had died out, nearly 40 percent of Yellowstone's 2.2 million acres had been touched by fire. The fires, however, didn't burn in a solid wall destroying everything in their paths. The fires jumped around, burning in a **mosaic.** From the air, Yellowstone Park looked like a **quilt,** with **black burned patches** stitched together with pristine **green patches.**

This Burns Me Up!

The fires in Yellowstone upset many people. They thought Yellowstone had almost been **destroyed.** Others, however, argued that the fires **helped** Yellowstone.

For many years, every Yellowstone fire—whether natural or human-caused—was **extinguished.** This was **park policy** because it was believed that Yellowstone should not change. Similar policies existed in other national parks and national forests, too.

In the 1960s, however, scientists realized that fire played an important role in Yellowstone's ecosystem. They said that fires cleared out dead wood, opened up spaces for new plants, put nutrients back into the soil, and helped animal habitat. They argued that fires had always been a **natural part** of Yellowstone.

Fire: Nature's Home Improvement

After an event like the Yellowstone fires, **nature heals itself.** By September 1988, grass shoots were poking up through the ash in the areas burned in July. By the summer of 1989, meadows—which had been blackened in 1988—were more luxuriantly green than those that had not burned. These renewed meadows provided additional food for bison, elk, moose, and deer. Blooming flowers attracted insects, which attracted birds.

The fires created many other benefits for Yellowstone's plants and animals. The burned plants released their nutrients into the soil, fertilizing the earth for the next generation of plants. Plant nutrients flowed into streams, helping more aquatic plants to grow. These plants in turn provided better food and shelter for fish, especially Yellowstone's cutthroat trout.

Old Faithful geyser erupts against a smoke-filled sky.

Let It Burn

Yellowstone **park policy** changed in 1972. The new rules stated that fires caused by people would be put out. Wildfires **caused by lightning** would not be fought unless they threatened human lives or property.

This system worked well. Fires ignited naturally with a lightning strike, burned, and then went out during a rainstorm. Those fires started by **human carelessness** were immediately extinguished by firefighters. Then came 1988, the summer of fire.

On televisions all across America people watched beloved Yellowstone National Park burn. Magazines and newspapers were filled with photos of towering flames and tired firefighters.

Many people disagreed about how to handle fire in the Park. Some disagreed with the "let it burn" park fire policy. Others said, "Wait, the fires were a good thing."

Lodgepole pines, groundsel, and fireweed

The Seeds of Life

The fires took a heavy toll on Yellowstone's many older **lodgepole pines.** Hundreds of thousands of these trees died. But in their dying, the lodgepoles actually provided the seeds for new forests.

Lodgepole pines need the **heat of a fire** (at least 113 degrees) to open some of their cones and release their seeds. As the fires burned the lodgepole pines, their **cones** opened and millions of **seeds** fell to the ground. After the fires passed, scientists found 50,000 to 1,000,000 lodgepole seeds per acre in some places! These seeds provided food for squirrels, chipmunks, birds, and other animals. The following spring, millions of tiny pines sprouted in the rich ash created by the fires.

Lodgepole pine cone and seedlings

The burned forests also enabled sunlight to reach the forest floor. Grasses, wildflowers, and shrubs now had a chance to soak up the sun and grow where, before, dark forest shadows prevented them from taking root.

Animals and the Fires

Moving On

From bears to bugs, the fires affected Yellowstone's wildlife in different ways.

Most **birds** and their young simply flew away to safety because the nesting season was over. The following year, however, eagles and ospreys suffered because they use the same nests year after year. Many of these nests were destroyed in the fires and high winds.

Larger mammals like **bison, elk, moose,** and **deer** grazed ahead of the blazes. **Black bears** and **grizzly bears** smelled the smoke and kept clear of the fires. **Coyotes, wolves, weasels,** and **squirrels** ran to safety ahead of the fires. Some **small animals** like **chipmunks** and **moles** simply stayed in their burrows while the fires passed overhead.

Thick smoke caused the most deaths among the large animals.

Moving In

After the fires died, the thousands of dead trees provided homes for **beetles, carpenter ants,** and **wasps. Woodpeckers** feasted on the insects and drilled holes for homes in the dead wood. Later, **bluebirds, chickadees,** and **swallows** moved into the old woodpecker holes.

By the summer of 1989, life had returned to almost every burned area—and so had human scientists, who came to learn all they could about the summer of fire and how nature heals itself.

Elk calf

FIRE EXIT

Historic Structures

The first **Native American** residents in the Yellowstone area lived in **tipis** or **wickiups.** Today, a few cone-shaped stick wickiups (shelters probably built in the 1800s) still stand in the Park. **Trappers** who came to Yellowstone built **log shelters** or lived in **tents.**

More visitors came to enjoy Yellowstone's wonders after it became a national park. Yellowstone was even nicknamed "Wonderland."

The early tourists stayed in tents. Before long, however, park visitors wanted more comfortable lodging. In Yellowstone's early days, several large hotels were built. Today, two of these historic hotels, **Old Faithful Inn** and **Yellowstone Lake Hotel,** are still enjoyed by guests.

Plains Indian tipi

Old Faithful Inn

Old Faithful Inn opened for business in 1904. For more than 100 years, millions of visitors have enjoyed staying at or touring the beautiful inn, which has withstood both fires and earthquakes.

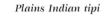

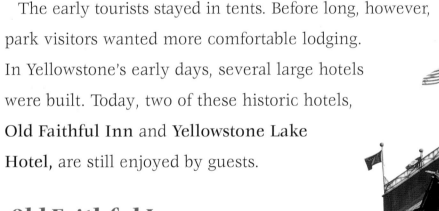

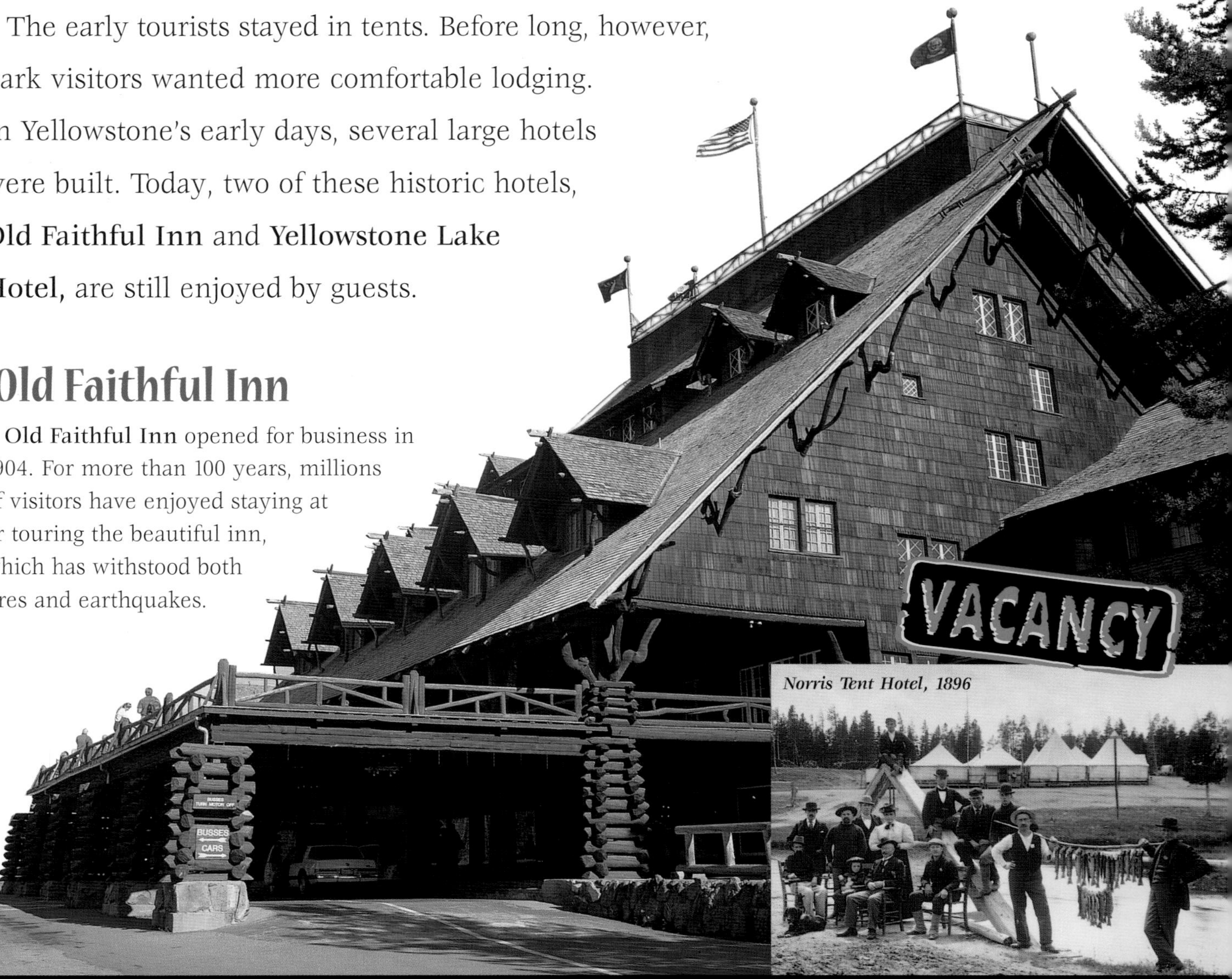

Norris Tent Hotel, 1896

Old Faithful Inn

Tick Tock goes the Clock

The huge clock on the fireplace is a manmade Yellowstone wonder. The iron clock is over 20 feet tall! Every two seconds the clock's "tick tock" can be heard by listening guests. Clock facts:

The clock is 20 feet tall.

The clock face is 5 feet in diameter.

The red Roman numerals are 18 inches tall.

The pendulum is 14 feet long.

The pendulum's disks are made of copper. The weights are iron.

The hands are each 3 feet long.

Until a new mechanism was installed, an inn staff member had to climb onto a narrow walkway and wind the clock.

In 1904, there were 140 rooms for guests. Two wing additions provided 187 more rooms. A room with a bath cost only $4.00 in 1904!

Old Faithful Inn bedroom, 1904

Old Faithful Inn is a unique historic building. The inn's architect, Robert C. Reamer, wanted the inn to have a natural look that fit into Yellowstone's scenery. The inn's tall gabled roof with its steep pitch was meant to "echo" the area's mountains. The inn was built of local Yellowstone materials. The walls are made of lodgepole pines harvested in the Park. The foundation is constructed from Yellowstone's volcanic rocks. Even the sand for concrete came from Yellowstone.

Visitors are impressed with the inn's huge lobby. Wood is everywhere—from pine log walls to beams, rafters, posts, staircases, and balconies. More than 10,000 logs were used in the lower story alone. The builders selected uniquely shaped logs for posts and railings. Hundreds of polished knots, rounded burls, and curved branches decorate the interior.

Most visitors crane their necks to see the ceiling towering nearly 77 feet above them. Long ago, visitors could climb up to the "crow's nest," a little tree house at the top of the inn.

Cleaning all of the inn's beautiful wood takes skill and patience. At one time, cleaners used long knotted strings of sheets, compressed air, and climbing equipment to keep the inn sparkling.

The inn's tall fireplace and huge clock also catch guests' eyes. The fireplace, 42 feet tall from floor to ceiling, contains four hearths, burns only lodgepole pine, and is built from 500 tons of Yellowstone rock. The fireplace is more than 15 feet wide. Rocking in front of a crackling fire is a pleasant place to chase away Yellowstone's frequent chilly days or nights.

Yellowstone Lake Hotel

Today, guests enjoy **Yellowstone Lake Hotel's** long porch, tall columns, and beautiful views of Yellowstone Lake. Once called the Lake Colonial Hotel, the current hotel stands where Indians, trappers, and mountain men once gathered.

The Lake Colonial Hotel opened its doors in 1891. In later years, Robert Reamer, the architect who designed the Old Faithful Inn, made many changes to the hotel, especially the long porch in front, the columns, and the spacious interior sunroom. Today's guests relax in the sunroom to play checkers and chess, enjoy music, talk, and gaze out over Yellowstone Lake.

Over time the hotel fell into disrepair, but was restored to its former glory by its 100th birthday in 1991.

The **Lake Ranger Station,** near the hotel, is a classic historic Park structure. Log cabin ranger stations like this one were built around the Park of local materials to blend in with their surroundings. The **Norris Basin Soldier Station** (now the Museum of the National Park Ranger), the nearby **Norris Geyser Basin Museum**, and the **Fishing Bridge Museum** are other fine examples of historic log cabin buildings.

Yellowstone Lake Hotel, 1904

Norris Museum

YES WE ARE OPEN

Yellowstone Lake Hotel

Roosevelt Arch

One of Yellowstone's most unusual historic structures is the stone **Roosevelt Arch** at the park's north entrance. This 50-foot-tall volcanic rock arch greeted Yellowstone's early visitors who came to the park by train. Tourists rolled through the Yellowstone's gateway arch in stagecoaches on their way to see the park's sights. Today, the arch has its own park—called Arch Park—where you can picnic and see historical exhibits.

President Theodore Roosevelt gave a short speech at the cornerstone ceremony saying, "The Yellowstone Park is something absolutely unique in the world...." Over 3,500 people came to the ceremony and to cheer the president.

If you visit the Roosevelt Arch, look for these words in the arch's keystone: "For the Benefit and Enjoyment of the People." These words are from the law that made Yellowstone our country's—and the world's—first national park.

In 1995, some **very special "visitors"** passed under the arch. Who were these special visitors? They were the first of the **wolves** (brought from Canada) to be reintroduced into Yellowstone National Park. Hundreds of men, women, and children came to see the return of the gray wolf to the Park— absent for many years. And the wolves came to stay!

↑ *President Theodore Roosevelt laid the arch's cornerstone in 1903. A time capsule, containing a photo of the president, a Bible, local newspapers, and other items, was placed under the cornerstone.*

↓ *Roosevelt Arch inscription*

"FOR THE BENEFIT AND ENJOYMENT OF THE PEOPLE"

The Wild West

Today you can enjoy a **stagecoach ride** just like in the olden days. The stagecoaches, called Concord coaches, are replicas of the stagecoaches first used to bring visitors into the Park from the trains. The horse-drawn stagecoaches make thirty-minute trips in the summer from the Roosevelt Lodge. Don't worry about stagecoach robbers today, although in the past bandits held up and robbed the stagecoaches! Your stagecoach will carry you to a Western-style cookout where you can get a taste of the Old West. Your pioneer grub is cooked over an open fire.

TALLY·HO!

"Tally Ho" stagecoach with passengers and driver Frances James "Happy Jack" Kelly, 1912

Fort Yellowstone

In the Park's early days, the government sent **Army soldiers** to Yellowstone to protect the animals and the tourists. The headquarters was established in the Mammoth Hot Springs area. At one time, as many as 400 soldiers were stationed at Fort Yellowstone.

Today you can see the red-roofed buildings the soldiers used before they left in 1918. There are the **officers' quarters, soldiers' barracks, stables, a guardhouse,** and **Soapsuds Row** (where the laundry was done.) Today the buildings house shops, offices, and the Park Headquarters. The **Parade Ground** is an open grassy field where the soldiers once marched. Today the Parade Ground is Yellowstone's only "lawn," and its lawnmowers are the elk, which keep the grass trimmed!

Home Sweet Home

When the soldiers left Yellowstone in 1918, twenty-two stayed on to become park rangers.

↑ *Machine gun squad at Mammoth Hot Springs, 1911*

↗ *Present-day Fort Yellowstone*

↘ *Fort Yellowstone*